Dear Reader,

Before my mother passed away, she had begun compiling the multiple poems and essays she composed over the last decade of her life into one collection. These works recount the joys and sorrows of raising children in a foreign land, pursuing professional success and bridging the culture of India to the American society where her roots were planted.

Her ultimate joy and fulfillment was to share these reflections with friends, family and her fellow members of the Illinois State Poetry Society.

It is with no greater pride that I present you with this compilation. My hope is that as you read her words, you experience her fearless honesty and immense altruism that I was fortunate enough to have witnessed throughout my life.

With warm regards,
Dharati Szymanski D.V.M., M.P.H.
(a.k.a. "Usha's daughter")

Poems and Writings

Dr. (Smt.) Usha Mahisekar

Table of Contents

Birth of Poetry	9
Soap	10
Autumn	11
143rd Street	12
Me and My Hairdresser	14
36	15
E. T. Tube	16
Directions	17
Printers	18
Waiting for Summer	19
Numbers	20
"Mommy, I don't want to do this!"	22
Car Wash	24
Haiku	25
Family Next Door	26
Alzheimer's	27
House	28
Boss	30
Good Bye	31
Grand Canyon	32
Communication	34
Pyxis Pyxis	36
Grandpa	37
Retirement	38
Summer	39
Fireworks	40
Mother's Day Mother	41
First person, Second person, Third person	42
Family Tradition	44
Brief Encounter	45
Bicycle	46
Human	48
Failure	49
Why Me?	50

Winter	51
Roof	52
Monitor	53
Thanksgiving	54
Love	55
My Sister	56
Caregiver	57
Family Vacation	58
Palos	60
Stopcock	61
Abandoned Houses	62
Rebound	64
Summer in Antarctica	65
Disney	66
Life Lines	68
Sit Down	69
Unseen Wall	70
Jacket	72
How to Save the Job?	73
Surgeon's Knife	74
Summer in Chicago	75
Pain	76
Flammable	78
Life	79
Doctor vs. Patient	80
Cinderella in 2013	81
Swing	82
Home	83
Change	84
Final Days	85

Birth of Poetry

Birth of poetry
can be anywhere
in the home or homeless
in the school or playground
in the library or sanctuary
in the shower or on the tower
in the quiet place or in ecstatic joy
in tears of bliss or grief
in sorrow or happiness
in good or bad
in affection or hate

It just catches that moment
And that's the poetry

(2/1/2010)

Soap

Mom says, "Wash with soap. Clean with soap"
I don't know who created soap

If all the fishes wash with soap
Ocean will be full of bubbles

How big of soap an elephant might need?

If birdie uses it, soap will be stuck in her feathers

To wash giraffe's head, I might need a long soap stick

solid soap
liquid soap

I think
no soap
no soap

Autumn

Let's welcome the Autumn
Though cold is there to come
Day will become small
Where all the summer gone?

Picture of colors will be there
Green, red, orange, yellow mixture
Ground will be covered with leaves, fur
They will follow the sunny summer

With it they will be gone too
No particular pattern which I knew
Scenery of nature is amazing
It is really God's thing

In these colors, children are colorful
Their faces are so artful
Trick or treat and candy colors
are the extra new actors

Then comes the gobble gobble
To meet the family annual
Thank you God, for all the blessings
During happy and sorrow things

Let's celebrate coming autumn
As a new person in same costume, coming again

(10/01/2015)

143rd Street

Looks like I am stationed on 143rd street.

God has picked me up from a small street
in India,
and dropped me on this street
the 143rd street.

Of all my life
This is where I lived the most
On 143rd street.

So whenever somebody asks me
Where are you from?

I say I am from 143rd street.
That's where I lived the most.

I floated from Homer Glen to Orland Park
Of course on the 143rd street
From 1977 I am on that street
the 143rd street.

Changed the first tire puncture
Of course on 143rd street
Accidents, traffic tickets, warnings
on 143rd street
I almost know every tree
and every house on that road strip.

I always question,
Why there is school and funeral home near each other
On 143rd street

I always compare how it was before—
Just the plane farmland on both sides
Then slowly subdivisions and
gas stations and stores popped up
On 143rd street.

Two lane, four lane, construction lane, sewer lane.
Oh my God! When it is all going to be finished?
On 143rd street

Ninety7Fifty looks beautiful
But still Randy's anchored in my heart.
On 143rd street

355 makes my life very easy
But I don't like the 143rd street become busy

I always play the mind games to myself
That Oh! There was nothing before.
I keep on playing these mind games
Again and again and again.
Of course on the
143rd Street.

My American life on 143rd street

(4/11/2010)

Me and My Hairdresser

Me and my hairdresser
We go back thirty years in history
Exchanges of each other's life
Children, memories, families, sorrows and happiness
Every visit is more than hair styles
It is the revision of life

Again and again
Life in styles
So many times I changed the stylist
But keep on going back to her

Maybe, it is the thread of moments
Brings me back to her again and again

(4/2010)

36

I can't believe it is 36 years
Brought each other some cheers

Carried each other's sorrows and grief
But did not even stop for a brief

Some days were good, some were bad
Some were sad, of course some were glad

Moments of joy and shivers
To our life surely it anchors

With each other's help
we made this path
a beautiful walk
of our unique life

Happy Anniversary, Narayan

E. T. Tube

Life saving
Life choking
Miracle
God's hand
Soul helper

Ventilator's appendix
trachea's extension
elongated breather
elongated nose
elongated mouth

But sometimes
blockage of communication
Hindrance to tell and talk
miscommunication
voice box stopper
helplessness
un-understandable

And sometimes
extension of body without soul
extension of life without life

So E.T. Tube --- is it a blessing or curse?

Directions

I think I am allergic to directions
Very very hard to pay attention
When I was little
Understanding my right and left
Made my life miserable

Earth is round
Then if I stretch my right
Very, very, very far
It will become the left

I know Sun rises in East
And goes down in West
That's enough for me
But if there is no sun in the day time
Then what happens to my East and West?
Oh my God! This is really a test
I really think I am allergic to directions.

Printers

I chose to write about this printer which is sitting on my left side. I think it is HP 8100. There were so many printers in my house before this one. They were from all different manufacturers –Cannon, Okidata etc etc.

Nowadays printers are so cheap. But oh my God! The cartridges are so costly. And then each printer has its' own special cartridge. (I still have one tape package for my type writer sitting in my house. I know it is of not much use. But still I am reluctant to toss it.) Previously there were just two cartridges –black and color. Now there is black and four or five different colors.

When I was little, if I needed faint color I just used to add extra water. Why something like that cannot work with this new printer? Every time I want to print something important, my printer has no sufficient ink. I think printer is playing game with me.

And about the ink, I still remember in first grade I took the ink bottle to the school. I had a pen like the penmanship pen with the nib on the end. Every two or three words I have to dip that in the ink bottle. Then when I was in the second grade my dad brought me a ballpoint pen. It was so surprising to me to see that there is ink in that pen and I don't have to dip it in the ink bottle.

Maybe in my family I might be the last one to use the ink bottle.

*this entry was a prompt from a creative writers group

Waiting for Summer

Is it winter halfway done
Or the summer half way waiting?
The deep Siberian weather
Made me think worst may be over

Whatever groundhog tells
May be not true for Chicago
Oh but,
The day is getting longer
Little more sunshine.

Cheer up
Even if Siberian weather comes back
I will say
It will pass over
And my summer will be here

(2/23/2014)

Numbers

Your numbers are normal
Yes! I look normal on paper.
But inside the body what is there you don't know.

When numbers get little wrong
You're searching for diagnosis
You can't figure out what is wrong.

Each wrong number shows many different diagnoses
So you think of multiple diagnoses, but not the one.
So you are given three or four different possibilities, to
point to each possible disease.

My number of pills increased.
Some in the morning, some in afternoon,
Some in evening, some at night.
Thank God they don't ask me
To take overnight.

Some once a day, twice a day, thrice a day.
Some just for one day, 5 days.
Some pills are life lasting.

So in conclusion in very, very early stage,
When disease is just budding out,
Doctors don't know
What is what.

When the lab tests come,
Doctors know the diagnosis and start the treatment.
But now fight between the disease and doctor starts.

Whatever weapons being used,
The effect of the war, the patient suffers.
By the same doctor different diagnosis said.
Your friend also knows that there is something wrong.

So early phase of disease, doctors don't know anything
Be your own doctor.
Chase these early problems.

"Mommy, I don't want to do this!"

Make your room clean
Keep the toys away
You get a quarter for that
Oh Boy! Quarter! That's good
Let me go to my room

Where do I start?
What do I do?
Forget it. Forget it.
I don't want to
I like my toys

Where they are?
Here and There
Everywhere
Anywhere I turn around
I see the toys
And anywhere I look
I see my little books
I like it that way

Oh! But what about the quarter?
I want that quarter
To get the gumball candy
I want my own money
I will put quarter, quarter
Quarter, quarter, quarter in the bank
I will grow the money like in the tank

When I will be sixteen
I will buy the car.
Really I need this quarter
Let me start collecting and collecting.

Oh Boy! Let me start
But I like my room as it is.
How can I please my Mommy
Ok! I will clean my room.
Clean up clean up
Let me start cleaning up

Oh my God!
Something moved
I am scared
I jumped out of the room
Called my Mommy and screamed,

"Mommy I don't want to do this!"

She is mad at me
She is forcing me to
Go back to room
I don't want to do this
She went in the room
Real snake was looking at her

(7/4/2015)

Car Wash

I am a car in the car wash
My owner has left me
My owner is watching me from the window

But when my owner washes me
And touches me, I feel so good
Looks like there is connection between him and me

Best of all
I still like to be washed by the rain
That is my heavenly carwash

Haiku

College will start soon
Bundle of joy going far
Courage, strength for both

Family Next Door

When we moved into new neighborhood
Did not know even what to expect.
Golf, new and big houses
Beautiful scenery.

But worried-
I hope there are enough children.
My little daughter should not feel lonely.

And slowly slowly
House next door
Became the family friend next door.
In those three girls, mine merged smoothly.

Dear Jim and Linda,
You are the backbone of this friendship
We do not talk much, but we share many family moments.

Thanks for your friendship.

Happy 60th Birthday, Jim.

Alzheimer's

I am somebody
In my own house
In my own state
They say I don't remember anything
So what?
This is my home
My life, my kingdom
I can do
Whatever I want.
In my own home
I can remember
Or not remember
I am beyond the state of understanding, remembering
World has no effect
Because of my behavior
I am cruising in this
State of forgetfulness
That's fine with me
I don't want to go
Somewhere else
Please let me stay
In my home

(5/2009)

House

I have a beautiful house. I love my house. One day my neighbor wanted to put a fence. And the fence guy marked the borders. I lost my sleep. The tree which I thought was mine for all these years belongs to the neighbor. I argued with my husband. (I didn't have guts to get angry at the neighbor.) After two days I was quiet. Sitting on my deck waiting there watching over the fence was a squirrel. I walked towards her and she disappeared under the house. I am thinking, "Ha ha, *you* are under *my* house." She must have said, "Yup, I lie under your house."

I start thinking, who are the people who live under there? I call all the things belong to me are people. All this time me and my husband were living in this house-unofficially it is somebody else's house. The squirrel, this rabbit who fights a war over my vegetable garden. He thinks I plant my garden just for him. As if he is my boyfriend or what? There were eight to ten sparrows sitting on the trees. I try to get them away and they are disappearing. I turn around, right away they come back. They are sitting on the tree at the root of the branch, then under the home.

So squirrels, rabbits, birds stay under the house. Inside you can catch them, under the house it is their kingdom. They are enjoying. But I pay the mortgage and they didn't have to do anything. They don't care about the boundary of the home. Sometime if I kick them out they will go to the next house without knocking the door or asking permission.

They are not hiding because they have no immigration card or green card or citizenship. They are citizens of the trees of this community. No government official takes them as issue at the election. These are the people not bad. In fact they are supporting the soil. Even if they did not read what Al Gore says about the environment, they are the environment protectors.

They don't create the junk like I do. No plastic use. No aluminum use. Everything is bio-garbage. Should I say they are superior to humans? Really they enjoy the beauty of nature and I am with the I-phone, T.V., cable, juke box, play box, fights and arguments. Look at the display they have. I don't see they fight each other. Lord had created them and they do their work quietly, achieve their goal.

After all this my mind was made that the neighbor's fence was also beautiful. It did not bother me anymore. It is just the mere border that is greater by count. In reality the whole world is one.

Boss

You are the Boss of Mahisekar kingdom.

You are loving Tata for Ravi, Linus, Seth, Hugo
And little Laurel.
You are kind Daddy of Sameet and Dharati.
You are Favorite Father-in-law of Sarah and Adam.
You are La Naa to Papi, Brother in law to Paul.

Laxminarayan to Temple
Mahisekar to social
Larry to KDK

You brought the inspiration to many people, relatives
Like Dhanraj and Dhanashree.
Your courage to land in US on your own
really admirable.

You are really the boss of everything.
And you are mine.

Good Bye

I shook his hand
Grip was weak but meaningful
Words were coming through the touch
I know what he said
Untold was told

I was not ready to accept
Being eldest in the family
Responsibility made me stand still
Prayers were not heard
Lots of sadness to bear

He never came back.
I guess
That was my last.

Good Bye, Daddy.

(6/8/2010)

Grand Canyon

I was at the Grand Canyon for a conference. There was a two hour lunch break. So I decided to take the helicopter ride. I went to the helicopter booth- bought the ticket. There were two Canadians, one Japanese person and myself. Helicopter started. We were circling the Grand Canyon. Pilot was talking and describing different parts of the Grand Canyon, their importance. All sightseeing.

And suddenly we could not hear anything. First we did not realize. We all four were unknown to each other. (Only we knew which country we are.) After some time we realize we can't hear anything from the pilot. There was no communication. Then after circling we saw the helicopter was getting down on one of the points on the Grand Canyon. Pilot got out and he said there is no communication with the main helicopter center. We looked all around. We were way, way, way high. There was nothing around.

For ten minutes we didn't feel anything but then we got scared. There was nothing to communicate with this whole wide world. Just the four of us and then the pilot. The pilot was telling us, "Don't worry, don't worry. Something will happen."

For a while we looked at the trees, collected some rocks. We were not in the mood to talk social to each other. After some time we took out our jackets and waved in the sky hoping somebody will see us. Somebody will find us.

That one hour in my life was really, really detached. Nothing attached to the world. Nothing attached to the people. Nothing, nothing. On that rock we were about an hour with no communication.

Then one helicopter saw our jackets maybe and our pilot said. "Don't worry, that helicopter will tell the main center." Then another helicopter came. Then we went in a different helicopter to the main station. But that one hour of my life I will never forget.

Communication

Talk talk talkers
Are not communicators
Communicators
Are not talkers

Communicate
Don't create confusion
Illusion or delusion
Find the conclusion

Eye to eye can communicate whole word
More than the unspellable big long word

Create a fusion of thoughts
No more clutter or clots
Talk heart to heart
Of course that is an art

Let heart touch the heart
Mind flow in the mind
Feelings flow in others

Let us mix in each other
Touch each other's hands
That will communicate million words

Are you scared?
Are you timid?
Are you selfish?
Are you confused?

There is nothing yours.
Nothing mine
Nothing anybody's

Please let it go.

Please communicate

Let the flow of life transcend

(5/1/2015)

Pyxis Pyxis

You may not recognize me
Who else I could be?
I am the same person
supposed to be

My finger is the same
My iris is the same

Look at my name
it is the same

Oh Pyxis! Oh Pyxis!
I am not from Texas

Open the door
Open sesame, Pyxis

My patient is waiting,
my frustration is growing.

Grandpa

Oxygen in my nose is ok.
Push my wheelchair near him
Oh God! Please bless him and me.

I have congestive heart failure.
I want to hold my grandchild in my hand soon.

Hey Doc, go ahead, give me lasix, dig & blockers

The joy of holding him in my hand,
Supersedes the side effects of your drugs
If your treatment can help me reach him,
That's the greatest fulfillment of my life.

Thank you Doc.

I don't care what happens tomorrow
But let me hold him in my hand today.

Retirement

To retire or not to retire
To be or not to be
More difficult question than Hamlet
Answer is USHA

U - Ultimate decision depends on
S - Satisfaction
H - Health
A - Availability of the $$$ in retirement

So when making decision
Remember

USHA

Summer

Hi Summer, how are you?
When did you come?

My garden buds coming out
The earth is warm
Weeds getting scooped out
plants getting planted
mulch getting spread out
water getting sprinkled in
Garage getting cleaned out

Oh Summer! Let me enjoy this
before you go out.
Please stay little longer

(2010)

Fireworks

Sparkling lights in the sky
With music synchronize the light
You can repeat same thing
Exact the same way
With modern technology

Oh
But God's firework is different
Like thousands of lightening bugs dancing together
If there is music also
That will be beautiful firework.

Look
It is thundering
Lightning in the sky
The dance of lightning every time different
Never the same again

Lightning is romantic kiss of cloud and earth
Under the umbrella of sky
Divine firework is God's grace

Therefore enjoy any firework
Celebrate Fourth of July

Mother's Day Mother

We don't talk much
but you love me as such
I wish somewhere
break this wall of silence
it be no more

Every time I start the conversation
you cut me off
Words will flow like river.
free, without holding back anything.

We may agree, disagree
like, dislike
but still need to talk each other.
I am thirsty for your words.

When you were in me
you were 100% mine
Now I will be happy
even if you are 1% to me.

Seems like everything is slipping away from my hand
For good or bad
all the pieces of the puzzle are getting together.

If that is called life
so be it.

(2006)

First person, Second person, Third person

Sometimes I talk to second person.
But that second person is the first person.
The second says to the first –
why are you changing the person?

No No No!
This is a grammatical person.
This is not a real person.
We are not changing any person.

That is not true.
I am a real person.
I am also the real person.
Now we both are talking about the third person.
Oh yeah! But the third person also is the first person.

You mean we all (the first, second, third person)
are the same person?
Yes! We are the same person
but in the three grammatical persons-
first, second and third.

How did that happen?
Yes- because I (first person) talking to you (second person) about her (third person).

Got it silly!

No No No.
I am talking to you in the mirror about a goofy girl
that happens to be me.

And as God is everywhere,
he is also in first person, second person and third person.

Family Tradition

Sitting quite alone
Looking through window
Reviewing my life
From India to America
I thought to myself
What is my family tradition?
I don't think there is any.

I am sandwiched between two traditions
One of my parents' and another of my children's
They are from two different cultures,
Countries and thoughts

Which one is good?
I can't decide.
Which one should I cling to?

Or should I take
Little bit of both?

America is melting pot of many traditions.
Any tradition which takes me near
Truth and satisfaction
Is my family tradition

(11/2010)

Brief Encounter

Intercom said "Anesthesia to emergency room, Anesthesia to emergency room". I ran with my two residents to emergency room. We ran different different corridors, cross the different different doors, change different directions. At last we were at the emergency room.

As soon as we enter the emergency room the secretary said, "Room 2, Doc". My resident ran there. I barely saw the people waiting in the hallway. Security telling the guy to sit for a while. He has slight receding hair, blue eyes, sharp long hair, tall, long tattoo. He is looking at the wall. I didn't know why but I captured his picture in my mind.

To the Room Two. My residents were there. The patient on the bed is there. No air. CPR was not successful. Sounds of life we did not hear. It was car accident with youngsters. This patient who is not alive was the carbon copy of my waiting picture outside.

Before even anybody go to the waiting room, I know that was the dad, praying to God, hoping for his son to be alive. But he was not. That dad's face til this day, I have never forgotten.

Bicycle

On my fifth birthday
I hope I get a new bicycle.
Nice red and yellow
Better than my old tricycle

My little brother
Eating there, popsicle
I will go in the neighborhood
Impress all the children

But will that be the gift better
Should I ask something smarter?
No, but I want a new bike
Old one is too small for me
Let me pray for new bike

Bike, bike please come
I will blow my bubble gum
In neighborhood I will be hero
But I have dollar zero

How can I get a bike?
Oh yes the idea strikes
Let me call Grandpa

Oh he is not home
He is gone to Tampa
I kept the message anyhow
Can he hear that now?

Bike came in my dream
She said we are the team
I will not leave you alone
To me till you own

I have no bike
It has no spike
I cannot take hike
My dog has no bike
I feel dog-like
I have no bike
I have no bike

Today is my birthday
But I don't want to play
Will my dream come true?
Something will happen I knew

Oh! Look there is new bike
At my door, which I like
Grandpa heard my message
We have great bondage

Happy Birthday to me!

(5/31/2015)

Human

My first name Human
Middle Name Denial
And
Last name Postpone

I like to deny whatever is bad
Instead of facing the reality which is sad

It can't happen to me
Maybe it is for somebody else

Beneath
It is chest pain
Or circling worries
Or losing job

And then
Whatever needs to be taken care
I like to postpone

(2/17/2011)

Failure

I ran for success
No matter where I got the access
Many times I was blessed
But sometimes I was very stressed

Failures made me surprised
To the extent I was depressed
Dark Nights, Gloomy Days
Wet eyes, staring gaze
Failures brought me to the bottom of Earth
To the empty life, nothing worth
Long tunnel without light
In the sky like a torn kite

I did not give up my dreams
I did loudly scream
On that failure ladder, I climbed again
Slowly slowly
Step by step
Carefully
Wisely
Watchfully
Correcting the previous mistakes

Failures gave me strength to succeed
Here I am back again.
Life is great
Enjoy the failures also
(9/27/2013)

Why Me?

Deep darkness, worries, tears are here
Nightmares are waiting to enter my fear

As doctor told diagnosis
My thinking stopped in stasis

In all people on earth, Why me?
Oh God! Whole life feels very gloomy

Tossing, turning, sobbing, crying
Will not help this lying, denying,

Surgery, chemo, radiation
But I am stunned at this station

Did I finish obligations?
My life is at difficult junction

Every minute on the clock feels so long
No matter what happens I should be strong

Let not this nightmare very prolong
Oh God! Hope the doctor is wrong

Winter

With December it starts
I should be really smart.
Dress up warm and cozy
I hope my nose is not rosy.

Inside to outside,
Layers after layers
I can't find my body
In these shivers.

North Pole is there.
Santa eager to come here.
Let me decorate the tree
So my house, Santa can see.

Tree ornaments twinkling
Star is auspiciously shining
Gift boxes are staggering
Tasty food is smelling

Earth is rejuvenating
White snow all covering
Trees are stronger than human beings
I am ready for hibernating

Reindeer are gone back.
Every day is weather check
To all those happy and healthy, New Years
brings in lots of fun and cheers.
I am waiting for March.
(12/2/2014)

Roof

If houses have no roofs
People look at the sky all the time
Count the stars

Sun and moon will visit daily
Enjoy the blue and white colors of the sky
Clouds will say "Hi!" to people
May be arch of the rainbow will peek in
Moonlight will be more romantic
Might feel close to heaven

Oops!
When snow will come,
Very cold wind ruffles in,
People will grow trees in houses
So they get some shelter

There will not be 2 story, 10 story or 110 story.
Everybody will be on same floor
No competition of how high
Or on what floor my house is.

Man will be more humble
In that wide open house
With sky as the roof

Monitor

Throwing all colors and numbers at me
Green, red, white, yellow and blue
Patient's life is balanced by these numbers

Looks like life is dancing through these colors
till a step is missed in the dance
And then the music gets louder and different

Of course the alarm goes on

(6/17/2010)

Thanksgiving

Change the meaning of Thanksgiving
People prefer going for shopping
Long lines for stupid sale
No fresh air to inhale

Midnight craziness
Make you careless
You spend your money
Is there remaining any?

Thanksgiving more important than shopping
Families need to be closely binding
Please stay home for Thanksgiving dinner
Family will be very much closer

Enjoy those precious moments
Pick up those happy remnants
Enjoy the value of Thanksgiving

(11/18/2013)

Love

Whenever I think of you, my heart beats very fast
I don't know about you, but I am really lost

Music pleases my silly heart the best
Music taught by you unlatched my eternal quest

You found the right keys to my desired innermost
But you are busy traveling from coast to coast

I wish I could break the chain of formalities
I have lost you, my dear, nearly several times

Without you my music slows and my life pause almost
Oh my love! Right now I want you to be at my doorpost

Until the end of my life I will anxiously wait
My love, my master, I hope it will not be too late

Oh God! Please tell me, why my love cannot be little rosy
Am I confused or has the world gone crazy

My Sister

My sister,
We travelled our long path together.
Sometimes we were away
But echo of our minds,
Ringing of our hearts
Glued us more
to each other.

I am glad that
God has let us enjoy
each other's company,
Share our sorrow and happiness.

I am so glad you are my sister
and my close friend.

Happy Birthday Papi
Happy Birthday Madhu

(2013)

Caregiver

I'm with her for couple of years.
Know her all moods, habits, tricks.
Sometimes we disagree a lot.
But still we work together a lot

Over time, not just the caregiver
Or relative but a real friend
Maybe God wanted me to meet her
Over time I learned the meaning of life
Much deeper, much broader, more thoughtful.

Now I know.

(11/24/2014)

Family Vacation

We were busy. Me and my husband were working hard. My parents were there with me. My sister joined me. Everybody settling down, my son and daughter growing up. They were in dance and sports and games and karate, etc. All these busy schedules of life- we realized we should vacation by ourselves-just the four of us. Everybody agreed but children put some conditions.

My son said parents will not decide where to go. Children will decide where to go. It was ok with us. Brother and sister became the team. Then they had arrangements. We all decided by rotation where to go. Big brother by five years thought he will decide all the time. But they would both decide where to go.

The children's second condition was they didn't want to go where we have friends. And if we have any relatives they didn't want to stay at their house but in the hotel. After much discussion me and my husband agreed to that condition also. (Of course all the expenditure belongs to parents only.) Children pack many things. Brother and sister were so happy. There onwards, every year, they took keen interest. We went to Seattle, New York, Boston, Pennsylvania, Williamsburg, Disneyland, LA.

Funny part is one year my son said he wants to go to Alaska. "Why you want Alaska?" I asked. "I want to go there for fishing" he said. That was his year to decide so we could not refuse. I inquired to Orland Travel Agency. She gave me package and cruise information. Price for four people was beyond my budget. I thought

"What were the children going to do in the ship?" Me and my husband never took the cruise before. He said we will feel seasick. I looked at the map. Flight was from Chicago to Anchorage. We were talking to friends. One friend said his friend's friends are in Anchorage. He gave their phone number. We politely called him and ask him, "Do the people there drive?" We did not know. We only pictured snow. "What do you mean do people drive? We have a highway" he said.

 So from Anchorage we drove to Fairbanks. See the road side-nice sightseeing. Then in Valdez my son went for fishing. That was his greatest enjoyment. When he came back at 10:00 pm he was so proud. He said, "Look Daddy, I caught the fish." And he caught a big halibut plus couple of small fish. And so the fisherman asked if he wanted to mount it. He said okay. Those three or four other small fish he put in the ice box. Ice box was covered. It was a round white ice box.

 Then while flying back to Chicago it was in the luggage area. I was worried if it gets tilted and water falls down on the next passenger. Oh my God! When we came home, my son ran to his friend. His friend's father used to take all these kids for fishing. So his friend's mom cooked the fish on that day. My son enjoyed that fish meal very much. Then after a couple of months one parcel came at the door. Until that time I had no idea what exactly mounting was. It costed something $7 or $10 per square inch. But we are into it so we paid it.

 And that halibut is still hanging in my family room on the wall. So when anybody talks about that halibut, it is the Alaska trip we remember.

Palos

Palos Heights, Palos Park, Palos Hills
Are these the towns of Paloses or palaces?
If so, then where are the kings of these palaces?
These are not palaces, but these are Paloses.
Palos is here and Palos is there.
Here a Palos there a Palos
Everywhere a Palos Palos
Ee ya ee ya oh
If it is "ee ya ee ya oh", then there should be a farm.

Oh yes there is a farm-children's farm.
On that farm is there a cow, sheep?
Cottages- oh yes
Church- oh yes
Art is there and quilt is there
Poetry is there and memoir is there
Literacy is spreading all over
Of course food is there

Children are happy
Farm is happy
Of course blessings are there
People are happy
And The Center is happy
Ee ya ee ya oh.

(5/19/2015)

Stopcock

Stopcock

3 way, 4 way

I wish life had a stopcock like that
I can do one thing at a time
and stop all other avenues of my life

I can switch around to
Whichever avenue I want to flow faster
I could stop the sorrows or pain –

Just by turning the stopcock.

Abandoned Houses

They are empty, faceless, but there is sense to it
They are looking at the world anxiously
for somebody to come to them

That abandoned house knows the whole story
of the persons who were there

Fight happened, homocide happened, she was killed.
He went to prison for life.
Children went to foster home. It was all part of life.

Nothing was the fault of the house.
That house is empty.

Look at the Pompei in Italy. Whole village was gone
 with natural disaster,
the houses are empty. Nobody there
for many, many years.

Look! When the mountains and earth and ocean churns
with whatever geographical calamities,
they say mountains came up and oceans went down
earth is seen.

But some houses were gone forever
floated or abandoned.

The water slides, mud slides in Bangladesh
separated people and houses

When you see these abandoned houses your heart stops.
What happened to those people?

House is the house. When it is lived in,
it is changed from house to home.
There is energy in it.

That energy is because of the breath of the beings-
whatever it may be
humans, animals, insects, dogs and cats.

But now nothing is there.
Just the spider webs

Water is gone
Heat is gone
Probably spider also does not want to live there anymore.

Please somebody come to this abandoned house.
Please please.
And make that house a home.

Thank you.

Rebound

I will rebound
What is rebound?
Go down and come up
I don't want to go down
I always want to stay up
Oh
That is not God's rule
When you go down you have no control
Going down is scary
Feary
Dark
Quiet
Horrible
Colorless
Deep down
I guess this is my journey
Then I will bounce back
I will rebound
After my chemo

(8/26/2012)

Summer in Antarctica

Maybe it is less cold than colder
Or little warmer than former
Everywhere windy white icy powder

Should we call it less colder than cold
Or may be little warmer than cold
Or maybe a degree higher than cold

Lichens and algae growing now
There more sun surfacing now
Less ice rocks are forming now

Look at those penguins coming now
Dormant life rejuvenating now
See that Nature's splendid beauty-Wow!

No matter how you say it
Or what you say it
Or what you think it

It is cold,

      very cold,

           very   very cold

Disney

I went downstairs, looked at the pictures sitting on the shelf and picked up the 14th picture. At first glance, I can't even figure out what is it. The picture contained lots of coins lying on a nice golden kind of tablecloth. But I don't see the table there. It is huge. People around look very small.

Then I realized it must be some kind of parade. And this is the float in a parade. I see my daughter standing on the ground and watching it. All the people in the picture are also staring at the float of the many many coins, some kind of Middle Eastern jars and hanging colorful red carpets. Ahh! It must be the Aladdin float. Is this parade from Orland Park or somewhere else? I am thinking and thinking. And on the sides on the top of the trees I see hanging, Santa's face. Oh! It must be Christmas time. There is no parade at Christmas time in Orland Park.

Where did we go at Christmas time and saw a parade this huge and nice professional float when my daughter was in grade school? I remember now. We went to Disney World and that picture is from there.

Another good thing happened on that trip. We were at the hotel later on. And my sister called us and told the good news. Her boyfriend, Paul gave her the ring. And they happily married thereafter. Next time Paul and Madhu come to our house, I am going to tell them this story.

*this entry was a prompt from a creative writers group

Life Lines

Words of life
became the sentence
then sentences
of course a life line

Life is not as smooth as a simple line

Look for those
in between lines
Gray lines
Oh yes!
Those in between lines–gray lines
gave the real meaning of life

And those gray lines,
did not make the life like a simple sentence.

We like simple lines,
But we have to live with
complicated, complex lines

True life lines

Enjoy life.

Sit Down

Mom said, "Sit down"
Little six month old me- I don't know what she mean.

Teacher said, "You can sit down now"
Thank God. I am embarrassed.

Boss said, "Have a seat, we need to talk"
I am scared to death

Caretaker said, "Sit down"
I don't even know what she is saying.

What she mean?

(8/3/2009)

Unseen Wall

There is a wall between you and me
Nobody knows but you and me
We talk sometimes- but that talk is not the talk
May be obstructed by this wall

Sometimes I think
Where this wall came from?
When this wall was built?

It must be brick by brick
Block by block
Piece by piece
Moment by moment
Day by day
Years after years

I don't even know when it got started
If I knew it was going to be this big wall
I would have tried to
break it
stop it
Obstruct it
Or not let complete it

I should have tried with all my efforts for it to not happen.

But I did not know
In the flow of life, I just swam with the flow of life

I just swam and swam
Just swam with the flow

I kept on flowing and flowing
And the wall kept building and building

That's ok
I will live with the wall

As far as you are ok and happy beyond this wall

Jacket

What are the seasons of Chicago?
Of course no monsoon here
Miss my childhood weather
From six seasons came to four
Spring, summer, autumn and winter

But they are only on calendar
Are they four really?
What a question oh silly!

Then came down to two seasons
Winter and summer
Winter and construction
Potholes or no potholes
Gardening or no gardening
Cold or not cold

Two are ultimate
Season of Jacket
Or season of no jacket

(3/26/2014)

How to Save the Job?

Work hard and make the boss happy.
That does not work,
Because boss is never happy.

Work slow and let the work fill the whole week
That will make boss very sick

Make sure you are needed
Even if the boss is greeded

When economy went down
And company is closed
It did not matter
How did you work?

Work what you love the most
Then it does not matter what is the just

Let the pieces fall
Wherever they belong

But try to save the job
if you can

(6/17/2010)

Surgeon's Knife

As the lightning strikes
I put the knife on the skin
Praying the God
I hope it is not Cancer
But if it is
Please give me the courage and wisdom
to take it out all
And let my patient enjoy
rest of the meaningful life

(7/2010)

Summer in Chicago

Summer in Chicago is a ting of fall in the morning
Ting of monsoon in the afternoon
Ting of autumn in the evening
Anything is possible in the summer in Chicago

We don't even know about one day in the future
These are the games of nature
We really appreciate these summer days
Before hibernating again in the winter days

(2010)

Pain

Oops!
Pain is a four letter word.
We teach not to say four letter words.
But this one we scream, tell everybody, seek for help
Use any possible remedy we hear.

Pain you cannot describe.
Doctor cannot see it.
I cannot see it.
You cannot touch it.
You cannot hear it.
You cannot smell it.
You cannot taste it.

Pain is not the tumor or lump I see it
There is no lab result for pain.
Doctor rate the pain 1 to 10
But if my pain is 100, then where his scale will go?
Maybe like Giraffe's neck.

Pain is subjective.
Some pain for you might be lot more.
Same pain for other may be ok.
You might need lot more drugs.
I might have learned to live with pain.

Drug companies making lot of money by so called pain.
If we don't have pain, then they will be out of business.
And that is their pain.

Pain can be nonverbal.
Face is the face of the pain.
Hand is the face of the pain.
Body is the face of the pain.
Behavior is the face of the pain.

Whatever it is
To some extent pain is good.
It shows where the problem is.
It is indicator of much diagnosis.

And pain is there.
Since life is there, pain is there.
Because of pain, humans are attached to each other.
They talk to, listen to and help each other.
Pain is the sign of humanity.

Please help each other.

(10/4/2014)

Flammable

I see the sign in O.R.

Flammable

    Anesthetics

        Prohibited

Mind goes back in history
Using chloroform
in small village in India
under the kerosene lantern

with God's grace
everything went on ok

That little miracle in now over forty years old and leading the nation

(5/2010)

Life

Life is there
Life is here
You cannot mold it
You cannot turn it
You cannot bend it
You cannot reverse it.

Sometimes meaning of life is in between the line
In the footnotes
Beyond the rules and regulations
Beyond the policy and procedures

Sometimes you can touch it without touching
Smell it without scent
Hear it without sound
Read it without eyes

Go ahead and live to the full extent.
That is the fun part of Life.

(2/2004)

Doctor vs. Patient

This passage is not about the patient against the doctor, not about the unhappy patient, not about any malpractice suit or view of the medical profession. This is about my views about my situation. The thing is in this story I am the doctor, I am the patient also, but I am not treating myself.

Let me make it clear. I am a physician. With beautiful hopes of doing many things, I retired in January 2012. Enjoyed for six months. Suddenly one day bomb shell fell on me. I was diagnosed with Ovarian Cancer. Of course doctors are not immune from any diseases. For God all human beings are same. He throws any disease to anybody depending on his wish of the day.

But we created prophylactic things in the society. There is preventive medicine. We tell patients don't smoke, don't drink. Okay. I never smoked, never drank. No drugs. Regularly exercised – of course sometimes as a human being I missed. If I did exercise seven days a week without fail I would not be human being... I think. Took care of my professional activities, social activities, volunteer work.

But ultimately, everything I chose to do and not to do –I chose not because someone said to do or not to do, but because I loved to.

Cinderella in 2013

In the world, there are many Cinderellas
With stepmothers and stepsisters.

Still this day, all Cinderellas working hard
Stepmothers may not be that bad

Stepsisters may be naughty
Sometimes they are guilty

Cinderellas dreaming for Prince Charm
They waited so long

Nobody clicked them
Carriage never stopped by

That fairy tale Cinderella gave false hope
To Cinderella in 2013

Fairy Godmother says,
That was a story
But this is life.
Life is adjustment

As far as he is not Prince Harm
Don't wait for Prince Charm

(7/12/2013)

Swing

You and me are so different
But on the swing are the same
Enjoying the life together
Laughs and laughs in the air
Are we friends or not?
Or just the strangers found the joy.
Yes, whatever may be the thing
You and me are the same
Of this moment of this joy
At this station of my life
Enjoy the life.

Home

When you ask me, "Where are you from?"
What should I answer?
In my mind raises the big stream of questions

You mean, "Where was I born?"
That is thousands of miles away
I hardly lived there.
Should I answer, where I went to school?
That has no connection to me much
Should I answer where I graduated?
That was just the youth years.
Should it mean from this country or other country?

I look back and I know
I lived here more than any other city in my life

The colors of Chicago
The seasons of Chicago
Have molded my life
Helped me to learn

After forty years of life here
Even if my footsteps started from another city

Chicago is my life and my home

(2010)

Change

Childhood to old age
Lots of changes

Life turns and twists
Through these many years

Walked through different paths
And sailed in many motions

Tried to catch the different moments
Still they slipped away, far away

Try to reach the next one
With many hopes everyday

We didn't even realize,
Every moment
brought a little change in us.

(9/2010)

Final Days

I read lot of Indian history.
During childhood I hated history.
Nobody made that subject interesting to me.

As I grew older and older
I started liking more and more
Maybe because I am slowly becoming
History in this wide world.

Came across British ways of handling
Kings and important people.
Many finished far from their beginning
Burma's king, finally rested in Ratnagiri.
Godse in Bhopal.
Last Chhatrapati of Kolhapur in Pakistan.
Bahadur Shah in Burma.

Even if his final days are in some other region or country,
Far from where he started
That person is never erased in God's world.

(12/29/2015)

www.ingramcontent.com/pod-product-compliance
Lightning Source LLC
Chambersburg PA
CBHW020622300426
44113CB00007B/748